Contents

Songs

Riddles

The hokey-cokey

You put your right arm in,
You put your right arm out,
In out, in out,
And shake it all about.
You do the hokey-cokey
And you turn around ...
That's what it's all about!

Oh, hokey-cokey-cokey,
Oh, hokey-cokey-cokey,
Oh, hokey-cokey-cokey,
That's what it's all about!

You put your left arm in ...

You put your right leg in ...

You put your left leg in ...

You put your whole self in ...

The big ship sails on the Alley, Alley, O

The big ship sails on the Alley, Alley, O,
Alley, Alley, O, Alley, Alley, O,
The big ship sails on the Alley, Alley, O
On the last day of September.

The Captain said, "It will never, never do ...

The big ship sank to the bottom of the sea ...

We all dip our heads in the deep blue sea ...

If you're happy and you know it

If you're happy and you know it,
clap your hands,
If you're happy and you know it,
clap your hands,
If you're happy and you know it,
And you really want to show it,
If you're happy and you know it,
clap your hands!

If you're happy and you know it,
stamp your feet ...

nod your head ...

wave your hand ...

shout "We are!" ...

I hear thunder

I hear thunder, I hear thunder.
Hark, don't you? Hark, don't you?
Pitter-patter raindrops,
Pitter-patter raindrops,
I'm wet through,
So are you!

I see blue skies, I see blue skies
Way up high, way up high,
Hurry up the sunshine,
Hurry up the sunshine,
We'll soon dry!
We'll soon dry!

The farmer's in his den

The farmer's in his den,
The farmer's in his den,
E ... I ... E ... I ...
The farmer's in his den.

The farmer picks a wife,
The farmer picks a wife,
E ... I ... E ... I ...
The farmer picks a wife.

The wife picks a child, ...

The child picks a nurse, ...

The nurse picks a dog, ...

We all pat the dog, ...

The grand old Duke of York

The grand old Duke of York,
He had ten thousand men,
He marched them up to the top of the hill,
And he marched them down again.

And when they were up they were up,
And when they were down they were down,
And when they were only half way up,
They were neither up nor down.

There was an old man called Michael Finnigin

There was an old man called Michael Finnigin,
He grew whiskers on his chin-igin,
The wind came out and blew them in again,
Poor old Michael Finnigin ...
Begin again!

There was an old man called Michael Finnigin,
He ate winkles off a pin-igin,
He grew fat and then grew thin again,
Poor old Michael Finnigin ...
Begin again!

There was an old man called Michael Finnigin,
He went out and made a din-igin,
His neighbours came and threw him in again,
Poor old Michael Finnigin ...
Begin again!

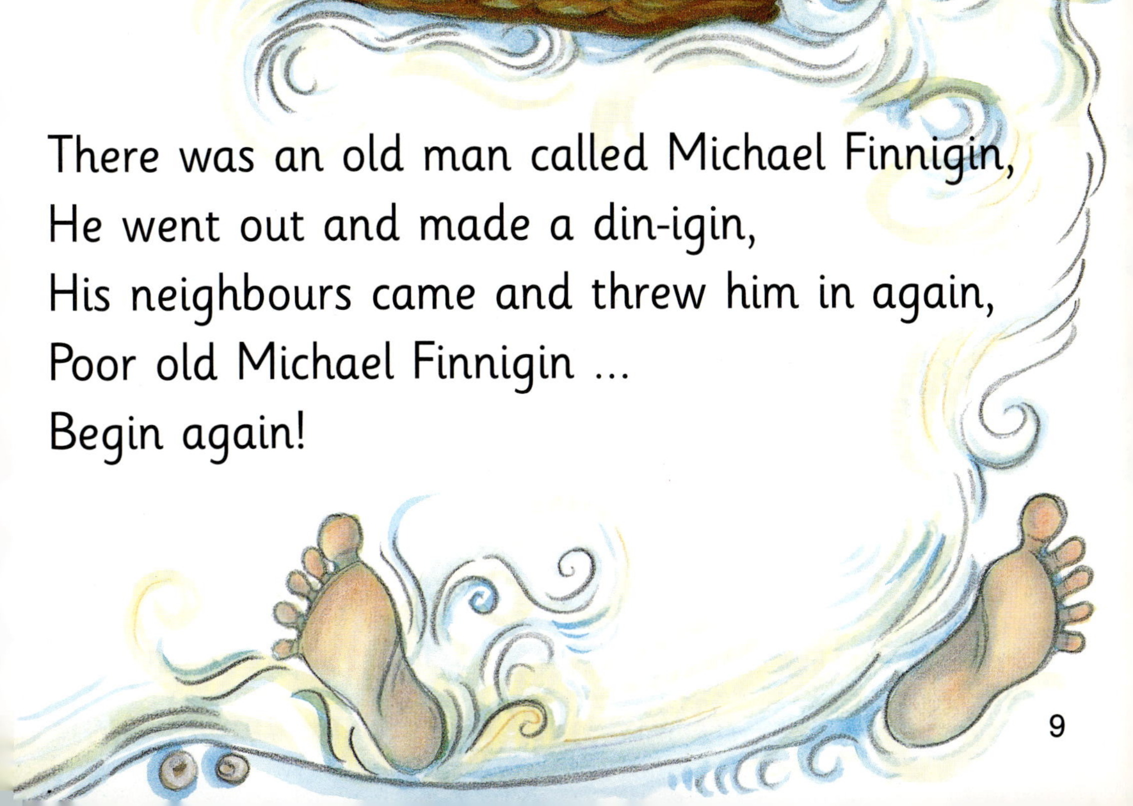

Old Mother Twitchett

Old Mother Twitchett has
but one eye,
And a long tail which she
can let fly,
And every time she goes
over a gap,
She leaves a bit of her
tail in a trap.

A needle and thread

I fly – like a bird

I fly –
like a bird,
And buzz –
like a bee,
Got a tail –
like a fish,
Got a hop –
like a flea.

A helicopter

Light as a feather

Light as a feather,
Nothing in it,
But few can hold it
For even a minute.

Your breath

Riddle me! Riddle me!

Riddle me! Riddle me!
What is that?
Over your head
and under your hat.

Your hair

Higher than a house

Higher than a house,
    higher than a tree;
Oh, whatever can that be?

The sky

Runs all day and never walks

Runs all day and never walks,
Often murmurs, never talks.
It has a bed, but never sleeps,
It has a mouth but never eats.

A river

You need me for sitting

You need me for sitting
Though I'm not a chair.
When you're running
I'm still there.
People say I'm soft
But I'm hard to find
'Cos wherever you look
I'm always behind.

Your bottom